13TH BALLOON

13TH BALLOON

A POEM

MARK BIBBINS

COPPER CANYON PRESS

PORT TOWNSEND, WASHINGTON

Cover art: Mark Bibbins

Copper Canyon Press is in residence at Fort Worden State Park in Port
Townsend, Washington, under the auspices of Centrum. Centrum is a gath-
ering place for artists and creative thinkers from around the world, students
of all ages and backgrounds, and audiences seeking extraordinary cultural
enrichment.

LIBRARY OF CONGRESS CATALOGING-IN-PUBLICATION DATA
Names: Bibbins, Mark, author.
Title: 13th balloon / Mark Bibbins.
Other titles: Thirteenth balloon
Description: Port Townsend, Washington : Copper Canyon Press, [2019]
Identifiers: LCCN 2019019606 | ISBN 9781556595776 (pbk. : alk. paper)
Classification: LCC PS3602.I23 A6 2020 | DDC 813/.6—dc23
LC record available at https://lccn.loc.gov/2019019606

98765432 FIRST PRINTING

COPPER CANYON PRESS

Post Office Box 271
Port Townsend, Washington 98368

www.coppercanyonpress.org

Why is there so much useless suffering. Why is there.

—Gertrude Stein

13TH BALLOON

As a house burns   sparks
land on the roofs
of houses nearby

Some of them also will burn
Some of them will not
Someone asks *Are there people inside*

      Sometimes there are people inside

They may walk out alive or be carried
out alive they may be carried
            in pieces they may
        be carried in bags they may
        be carried in smoke

Others in dreaming may wonder
whether they ever will wake
from the endless dream of sparks
clinging to their roofs
floating through their windows
landing on their beds

///

A few months after you died
I came home on a black and freezing night
to find a small cardboard box
on the steps outside my building

I opened the lid and inside
was a single newborn animal
hairless pink and clean
a rat a guinea pig I couldn't tell

Was it moving   I don't remember now
why can't I remember that now
It can't have been moving
it couldn't have
been alive
I considered my cat   asleep
in my apartment   would he
kill this creature if it lived
Did I have any milk
and how would I get any milk
anyway inside this tiny thing
that surely could not be alive

What kind of person
might have come and left
a baby possibly dead
animal there in a box
on my stoop   what kind

If this was a test I failed it

I carried the box
three long blocks
to the river and threw it in

I have never so much
as in the moment the box went under
the surface of the water
      stabbing and stabbing and stabbing itself
      with the moon's million obsidian knives
wished that I were dead

If death is a test I fail

If death is a test I pass

///

During the storm your ashes drop

out of the sky in clumps

and birds with sutures for eyes

peck the outline of your silhouette

onto the trunk of a petrified tree and clouds

shit mud on the sheets at night

and the trees piss phlegm and weep blood

that covers the ground and we slip and we crack

open as faceless birds descend to drink

as they hideously flap their hideous wings

and gorge themselves on ashes and pieces

of teeth and fragments of bones

that once were yours

Featherless birds dive into the furnace

where you burned

They swoop in and out of the windows

of hospital rooms and heavily horribly swirl

against what could be clouds or could

be the ashes of others we've burned

until the last of the birds engorges

itself on so much of your death that finally it

bursts like a boil in the sky

///

What might anyone have made
of you and me as babies
born into the mess and ferment
          of the late 1960s
Working-class babies born to parents
          who themselves were babies
          during World War II
Were they worried already
about Vietnam   or about some other
monstrous hand that would grab us
from our cribs by our feet
and throw us
into the war that would be
the war after that

They could not have known
that our war   because everyone
                          lands in one
would be with a virus   or that one
of the hands that failed to close
quickly or tightly enough around
it to stop it from killing you
would also belong to the state

At the beginning of every war
every baby is replaced
with a picture of a baby

In every eclipse the sun

is replaced with an x-ray of the sun

///

A person I knew for a short time
a short time after you died
guessed incorrectly that I would sleep
with him and furthermore that I slept with
a copy of *Bartlett's Familiar Quotations*
next to my bed   Though wrong
on both counts he was right
when he said I blushed absurdly
                              and too easily
but when I told him about you
he was taken a little aback
perhaps surprised that I had lived
through anything

I should remember now
what Velvet Underground song
after I turned him down
for the last time he left
on my answering machine in order
to convey that I was no
longer worthy even of his disdain
          I never told him the book
that was next to my bed was the copy
of *The Selected Poems of Frank O'Hara*
you had given me before you died

Yesterday someone told me that Frank's friend
the painter Mike Goldberg had died

and from here I can see myself

in my tenement room

on a night more than two decades gone

opening to Frank's birthday ode to Mike

when I reached down

to the floor next to my bed

to pick up the book that had been yours

///

Since you died the house style could best
be described as leaves that cling
to trees too long into winter
                    I understand how
                to miss a hint
as I regularly watch the anger
harbored against queer people inflate
like innumerable soap bubbles
in what passes for real time   A truce
can soothe for as long as it lasts
and the extent to which it's meant

            I set foot in a jungle once
                            so I know
how things on Earth can work
There were fewer animals than
I expected but I did see some
leafcutter ants and I climbed
an ancient pyramid and may
have heard a monkey
before returning to the lot
where the bus had dropped me off

Near the gas station some children
were taunting a dog
with awful mange

On the way back
to the beach town where I was staying
a unit of young soldiers
stopped the bus to search
for whatever a soldier searches for

I remember their rifles and their boots
and their silky eyelashes and that they
looked like children to
me then
        To whom must they look
like children now

///

Scraps of magazines
hoarded by boys
in our fort in the woods
The pictures were what   nude women
cavorting in a gym
nude women lying on a tile floor

I told myself not to look
at the boy next to me
in the horny grim leaflight
as he studied page after seedy page
I told myself   don't wish
for us to be nude together now
nude in the branches   nude in the clouds

Don't look at the other boy
in case he sees me looking at him
          Look down at the dead leaves
on which are projected
nude photos of me   nude photos of him
nude photos of him all slippery with me

Don't look for the two
of us nude on the rocks
where the sunlight cuts through
          the two of us
nude at the edge of the stream

Don't look at him   don't look

don't look at his hand   at his crotch

better to look at the ground instead

///

When I was a teenager I smugly told
one of my teachers I wasn't worried
about going to hell
because all my friends
would be there too and she just
as smugly responded
Yes but you won't recognize them

Now when I ride the escalator
to hell I have to kiss
everyone on it
even the drug lobbyists
      but we're all fine now
            very wealthy down here

Drop a kiss on the floor of hell
the three-second rule applies

          I may not care who
      I'm kissing anymore
          but neither do they

Hell is full of delicious flowers
and we keep scooping out
deeper hells for their decapitated stems

How cold could I have been to have said

that this is the way Celan ends

Celan ends Celan ends

      not with a bang

but a river

Woolf too   I mean

wind any creature tight enough

pull any creature loose enough

it does what it has to do

Still the flowers   I can hear them

are singing   *Don't leave*

you haven't finished

eating us yet

///

You and I never called each other
by the name we shared
It would have been like eating an echo

        each of us checking

      opposite sides of a two-way mirror

      for fog left by his own breath

Months after you died I saw someone
in a nightclub in a different city
than the ones in which our story crossed
itself out

      someone who knew us both

      but as it turned out

      not very well

He looked shocked to see me
a look I didn't need him to explain but

      Holy shit   he said

I thought you were dead

We celebrated my notdeath with shots
of something too sweet   and an hour later

      I was vomiting

into a mop bucket
in a corner of the club

The coelacanth was believed
to be extinct for millions of years
until the sea coughed one up

off the coast of South Africa

after a great storm

Its name comes from the Greek   *koîlos*

meaning   *hollow*

///

One of the only facts I can find
online about you is wrong

You didn't die on a Saturday night
you died on a Tuesday
It was a Tuesday morning the sun was frozen
and Mars or Venus barely glowed somewhere
or Mars was hidden in Tuesday
or Venus had broken into a billion splinters
of ice and covered the grass
outside the hospital
and the sun dragged with it your death
from the frozen pit
out of which daily it rises

Unless I too am wrong and Thursday
was the day
the nurse called and told us *It's time   you should*
come now he's getting ready to go

Ready to go   after how many times we thought
you were going   or were ready
to go or had gone
                    after how many times I'd arrive
                    at the hospital
thinking it would be the last
only to find you
sitting up doped up cockeyed grinning

You'd lift your head a little

and say *Hey what'd you bring me Boo*

and I'd climb into the bed

with you and say *Nothing good just me*

/ / /

William S. Burroughs said cut
into the present and the future leaks out

When I cut into the past
what leaks out is you

///

I grew up nowhere

near a sea   We had swamps

and ponds and creeks

and deer and jays

and every now and then

we'd find perhaps the tracks

of a fox in the snow

but no sharks   no jellyfish

no rays burrowing in the sand

        When we are young we wish

with uncertain fervor

                for what is not at hand

The first time I kissed a man

I was seventeen and he turned

out to be a minor criminal

He said his name

was Rich   and whether true or not

                it seems at least fitting now

Where he grew up

who knew for sure

the South   or so he said

which was also where the army

put him for a while instead of jail

for forging checks   or so he said

But before he told me that

        he told me he was bi

and his drawl made him sound

like a handsome sheep   *bah*

The kiss was real at least

One night he'd said we should pull

into someone's driveway

as I drove us home from the mall

where we stood bored in stores for hours

and called it work   I bobbed

in the fading waves

                  of that kiss for days

The first time I saw the ocean

I was twelve and the body

of water was technically a sound

Connecticut   January   freezing rain

I could only see a few yards

through the fog that turned

everything gray as a sock

        Alongside a breakwater

lay a tangle of garbage

and next to that the black

and brown back end

of a German shepherd

sticking out of the sand

///

We didn't have a word for us but what
could have been the word for us

Not lovers
though we loved

Not boyfriends   though we were
friends and still
boys in most ways when you died

Not partners   though we parted

These last two   I realize
are false cognates
the first of which derives from sharing
the second from taking leave

I have only language for you now
a language
                    that morphs like a virus
to elude   to survive   to connect
but I still don't
have the word

///

Come on stage and be yourself,
The elegist says to the dead.

—Mary Jo Bang

From here I can see a fountain
and a statue of a president
against a backdrop
of not yet spectacular oaks and maples
      rows of your friends
      in white folding chairs

Whatever flowers would still
have been thriving in the park
in the middle of September
I'm sure we were grateful for

When it was my turn
to speak at your memorial
what did I say
a version of   *you aren't really dead*
or *see you again*   some useless thing
any other deathstruck boy
lightly educated at state and city schools
might have said

Had I the gift of song I might have sung
as another friend sang
an optimistic Irish song

Afterward we collected
the chairs to take back to the restaurant
from which we'd borrowed them
and where you used to work

We turned off the microphone
and wheeled the podium away

Is there any song and if there is
what is the name of the song that goes
> *Now I am your widow*
> *who never was your bride*

///

One afternoon you fixed me
lunch in your tiny apartment
  cream of mushroom soup

  from a can

  and English muffins

As you set our bowls
on a blanket
on the floor because you didn't
   own a table
you put on
a bad British accent and said
We're having crumpets

It was raining but there was
an abundance of light
coming somehow from a source
outside we couldn't see
From here that light feels like
what music sounds like
just before the record skips

///

What is it they say about water

something about it seeking itself

and how did jokes like this one move

so quickly through the world in 1983

What's the hardest thing about having AIDS

Convincing your parents you're Haitian

Did they spew out of fax machines

were they blurted over happy-hour beers

by somebody's uncle

who worked for the state   or by another's

brother who worked in a garage

their jokes attaching themselves like leeches

to the swollen host of suffering

ugly but not useless

in order that we might endure

whatever side of suffering we're on

What does GAY stand for

Got AIDS Yet

How many other acronyms crossed the membrane

that separated my rural high school

from the rest of the world and entered

the gym one afternoon

and filled it like a syringe   Which boys

among us had just been watching

our friends in the showers

imagining their bodies

sliding against our own

like water seeking our own water

Which boys then saw the word AIDS

on the blood-filled test tube

on the cover of *Newsweek*

while other boys hooted and passed

the magazine around the locker room

Its own level   that's what water seeks

and which of these boys

was it only me   which of us

among any of these boys thought

now I know   now I know how

I'm going to die

///

When finally everyone was granted their childhood
wish for invisibility   it turned out to be less
erotically useful than we had expected

      The first legitimately wild desire I had
I turned into a pony so I could tame it
      He clomped for years among the precincts
of my visible youth   refusing
to be ridden   My use
of the word *first*
also proves to have been based
on an unfounded sense of possibility
that defines my fading generation still

We cannot measure
adequately the corruption of our age
but we can make the wet of it wetter
by diving into a lake
      the heat of it hotter
      by leaping onto a pyre

On hearing the kvetching of coyotes
in a graphite night
my doppelgänger climbs
into a constellation two feet off the ground
      When light
and death both want us
one of them might not
get its way

Other kid wishes were

        x-ray eyes

              the gift of flight

                    unending life

I've given names to a dozen more
wishes but deleted those names
because who could they ever have saved

Not the impossibly sweet and recalcitrant pony
who tried to steer me away from death

        however my death was trying to happen
whether by fucking or hiding
whether by drowning or by stars

///

Before we met   you had moved to Manhattan

but then you moved back

to the crappy capital that birthed us

How many of us did this

floating up and down

the Hudson like little Moseses

who couldn't make up our minds

I want to say you wanted

to be near your nephew

but maybe that wasn't it

In New York you met Val Kilmer before

he was famous   maybe you worked

in a restaurant together   anyway he gave you

a pair of his shoes

I still have them

and when I wear them

nothing magical happens but maybe

sometimes it does

William Basinski made the truest piece of art

in response to 9/11

before it happened

and mostly by accident   He had been

digitizing old tape loops

and as they played

the magnetized coating

on the surface of the tapes began

to flake off

to disintegrate   He kept recording

until there was no sound left

and replayed the digital files on his Brooklyn roof

as the sun went down behind

the appalling cloud of smoke

It's a good story   the one about

Val Kilmer giving you his shoes

I tell it when I wear them sometimes

           Oh these shoes

were Val Kilmer's   He gave them

to my dead boyfriend

when they worked in a restaurant before

one was famous and the other was dead

           Maybe not the best

story for a party and I don't often

dance where I might be caught dancing

although the shoes

look like they would be amazing

in that kind of motion

Did I say the shoes are white

      and that the beige lining

inside the soles has gotten so brittle and cracked

that each time I take them

from the closet and turn them over

a few more flakes fall out

///

Imagine a bird who lays her egg
then picks it up and flies without
landing until it hatches
Imagine a thousand
of these birds chopping away
at the soggy light

Since you died a thousand birds
have daily flown through me
each leaving behind an egg
          some of which rotted
some of which hatched
releasing more birds that pecked
at my skull
          but not generating the noise
          and pain one might expect
                    It's more like hearing
          someone typing
          an endless suicide note
          in a room at the end
          of a carpeted hall

Always one egg remains in me intact
and each time I yank it out
each time I crack it and crush it and throw
away the shell
          it reappears whole

I pull it out and pull it out

I break it a thousand times
but nothing is ever inside

I carry it and carry it   I do not land

///

I have been terrified
of clouds
since learning how much they weigh

A dam collapses
but there's no flood
the water already gone
presumably into a cloud

C.D. Wright said that elegy is a site
                    of *not loss but opposition*
nevertheless if anyone asks me
about death I try
to be optimistic   I say yes
there is death

For me elegy
is a Ouija planchette
        something I pretend not to touch
as I push it around trying
to make it say
what I want it to say

///

Seventeen years after you died
I sat with a friend on a Fire Island beach
after midnight drinking
red wine out of red plastic cups

Upon noticing in the distance headlights
bobbing in the fog I popped up and said no way
I'm forty same age as O'Hara let's go let's not
be this emergency again

It was a joke but it wasn't a joke
I knew what it felt like
to be of a generation fully
accustomed to being struck down

///

You and our friends hid from me
how sick you were
so that I might come back to you
      On its face
this strategy worked
though it didn't have to

You came to Manhattan
to visit me once while you could
still manage the trip
At the apartment of a friend
who was a designer
she took pictures of us
holding sunflowers and wearing her robes

                I loved playing for you
her answering machine greeting
which was just her purring her name
followed by a pause and
Do leave word
It possessed an elegance and brevity
we aspired to   though we knew
by then that your life was turning
into a sort of treatise on brevity

On the way back to my apartment
we saw a painting discarded
on the street and you said

the canvas was big enough

to wrap a body in   at least

that's what one

of us might have said

///

Here in the spectral academy
here in the home of the freaks
I devote myself to something
Candy Darling said

I will not cease to be myself for foolish people

       Yes but Candy what
       if foolish people's who I *am*

As the windows in the city sweat
             Candy's ghost collects
      herself behind one of them
      I know it
running her lines
her voice a raft
of white flowers floating
in a bathroom sink

Each day the internet invites us to try
suicide by zoo animals
or by eating a handful of ghost peppers
thus triggering a laugh track
over footage of a rainforest being razed

          Ruin feasts on us
pausing between bites to baste
us with our juices

As a stopgap against never praising

ruin enough we might praise the alien

We might

praise blood

We might praise the blood of the alien

            as it sizzles through the floor

while we're sat safe in our seats

in the theater of money

We must believe   as the child

in its nightlit room believes

       it cannot be seen

that nothing could touch us there

///

Inverted wooden tables   out of which

sprout the tenderest grasses

A blouse made of thousands

of needles

A chair   another chair

a dozen chairs

     a chest of drawers

all cemented in cement

Who will reach across

     a distance so great

     that light cannot cross it

to find a form for pain

Shoes of disappeared women

hovering in holes in walls

and sutured into boxes

of translucent animal skin

Enough rose petals stitched

together into a shroud

that it could cover

a hill where roses once grew

///

Not often but sometimes I look

at your photo album

a black faux snakeskin affair

Here you are

at football camp twelve

years old sitting next to Joe Namath

Here you're in school

standing in front of a bulletin board

to which are stuck letters that crookedly spell

WHAT IS DECEMBER

Underneath that is what appears

to be a poem I'm glad

I can't read

Your mouth is fully open belting

out something

a cheer a poem a song

Did you like to sing of course you did

like the time you sang

once from the hospital bed

Rich relations give crusts of bread and such

You can help yourself but don't take too much

There's one with you

and your siblings and a collie

who could be missing

one of its ears

You were born in an April

and you died in a September

It's a fair question but now I couldn't

say with much confidence

that I know what December is

only that you lived

through twenty-four of them

and then no more

As kids we were warned

against playing with gender

as if it were a plastic bag

THIS IS NOT A TOY

but here are some pictures

of you in drag

getting ready to head out to a party

or maybe that *was* the party

I think you were being Shelley Winters

You told me how you'd met her

and even went to her apartment once

When she flung open the door

she had scotch tape on her face

and her makeup half on

She was going to let you watch

her finish the job

and as she led you inside

she bellowed   *Come on*

you're in for a treat

///

Primula veris   Syringa vulgaris

Forsythia suspensa   Daucus carota

Asclepias syriaca   Centaurea cyanus

and *Toxicodendron radicans*

were among the things

that grew wild where I grew up

most more lovely in the woods and fields

than their Latin names

except for the last   poison ivy

some of which nearly every summer

I would accidentally touch

thereby prompting the publication

      of the story of my foolishness

      on the skin between my fingers

When one boy came to school

with his hands swollen so badly with it

that he could barely hold a pen

I was seized by a need to make

visible on my body

a difference about myself

I couldn't yet articulate

so I rode to the top

of a hill where I knew poison ivy

grew and left my bike

on the side of the road

while I rubbed the leaves as hard

as I could on the backs of my hands

Two weeks later they were still

weeping pus as I plunged them

into bowls of ice water   Even after

the rash abated they looked

mottled and dead for months

cowslip   lilac

forsythia   Queen Anne's lace

milkweed   cornflower

Another year   on the day

of class photos

I scratched at my face

with a sharpened popsicle stick

no blood   just a few pink lines

that didn't read

What else

I wanted a cast   on my leg or anywhere

I wanted braces and glasses

and my tonsils out

I wanted scars

I don't know when

or whether I figured out the difference

between wanting to be damaged

and wanting to be healed

///

The night David Wojnarowicz died

a spontaneous parade

clattered down Second Avenue

past the restaurant where I was working

my way through college

My syllabi were stuffed with books

about the plague

  Sontag's *AIDS and Its Metaphors*

  Monette's *Borrowed Time*

though all I had

to do to see it was to step

out into the street

In one class we were quizzed

on the five stages of grief

In another I was invited

by the instructor to stand before

a lecture hall full of nursing students

to field their questions

about the consistency of semen

more slippery than sticky *at least at first*

  Though not what most would call

  an expert witness

  I knew a thing or two

For weeks I sat at a table in a corridor at school

offering students condoms

in exchange for filling out surveys

about their sex lives

      I interned

with social workers in the AIDS unit

of a hospital uptown

where one afternoon a patient

lurched at me for a kiss

while dragging behind him his IV stand

which held aloft what looked

      like a bag of milk

Another afternoon

the head nurse gathered us

in one of the patients' rooms

to wait with him in the dark for his death

Was it that the room had no windows

or that the shades had been drawn

or is it my memory overlaying

that scene with a different darkness now

Either way how would his soul

      little ounce   the soul I barely

believed in then   escape

      I don't know what any

of this prepared me for   I don't

      know how anything escapes

///

Twenty minutes ago I learned
and promptly forgot
the Italian word for watermelon

The news is scrolling by
on a silent TV screen
and isn't even language anymore
just a digital river of trash

It's a symptom of living
in danger that my first
response is not to realize
how dangerous this is

I'd rather think of a man
on a verdant hillside
sprinkling salt on the flesh
of a slice of *anguria*
and the image   if not the word
is beautiful enough for now

There's a song we know that tells us
beauty's where we find it
but tonight I'm sure there's even more
where we left it

///

The opposite of irony is not

sincerity   it's hopelessness

Speaking of which I was struck

by how handsome

one of the commuters stepping

over us was as I lay

with ACT UP on the floor

of Grand Central Station

at 5:07 p.m. on January 23 1991

and how effectively that handsomeness

seemed to amplify the anger

in his eyes

       Everything about him said he would

be perfectly happy to kick any of us

in the head

for interrupting his timely egress

       to Westchester

but he was well enough versed

in the ways of rage

to know what would have happened

       if he'd done it

Only now do I recognize the humor

in ACT UP dropping over the arrivals board

a banner that read

ONE AIDS DEATH EVERY 8 MINUTES

and that I was lucky to have the luxury

of deciding not to get myself

arrested that day

Today is March 30

the thirtieth anniversary of ACT UP

and tomorrow Gilbert Baker   the man

who created the rainbow flag

                                        will die

Strange not to know whether one's life has

an asterisk hanging next to it

or is itself the asterisk

Strange to look vainly for oneself in history

and stranger to realize

that there is a chance

one might find oneself there

///

In some ways our story amounted

less to paper

than to staples   and holes

Only hours into the weekend you left town

with someone else without telling me

I sensed what it meant

Having swallowed

long ago the placebo of monogamy

I determined not to speak to you again

let alone forgive

I have no idea how much time passed

maybe a year

Now and then our friends would try

to convince me to see you

but I managed to avoid you

even in our shriveled city

and we would not talk again until you called

to tell me you had tested positive

I remember the weight of the phone

in my hand and thinking as I looked

out my window at the simmering

oranges of dusk above the trees

that *crepuscular* was one of the ugliest words

I could think of

though later it would be surpassed

by *cryptosporidium   histoplasmosis*
and *non-Hodgkin's lymphoma*
your official cause of death

I could say I started forgiving you that night
you called and maybe I did but before
me lay two interminable weeks
of waiting for my own results
during which I decided
I would leave behind among other things
this miserable stagnant city we shared

Eventually I and everyone around you
would be all but delirious
with forgiveness and mercy and love

What was that trick
How did you do it

It was as if you'd unfolded a map
you'd secretly been drawing
for us all along   a map
of a new and radiant country
across which together we would
carry you as you died

///

In truth I don't have that many

        memories of you left

        maybe enough

        that were they spliced together

the result would be the length of a movie trailer

or if weighed

would weigh as much as an eggshell

I can remember some things you said

if not verbatim   the tone   the inflection

and whether they arrived through a phone line

or through the air

or whether you thought something

you were saying was funny

like the time near the end

when you told your favorite nurse

who was trying a new diet

that if she really wanted to lose

weight she should have sex with you

      C'mere lemme stick it in you

      you'll lose thirty pounds real quick

We lived on a planet of disaster

We lived in a country of misery

We lived in a state of horror

We lived in a city of scandal

We lived in a house of daily dying

from which to distract ourselves

we sometimes embroidered

the filthiest jokes we could think up

on every available towel   pillowcase   sheet

I shouldn't say it saved us

but in many ways it did

///

I remember doing this once as a kid

watching a mosquito land on my

forearm then making a fist

after it stuck its sucker in

the muscle fixing it there on my skin

as my blood persisted in filling

the insect's abdomen until

it finally ruptured

leaving a smear

of my blood on my arm

Instead of *arm* I first typed *art*

I tried changing it and changing it

and changing it again

Now I don't know what to do

///

There are many ways to get

across a moat   I myself have

tried to swim and drowned

every time   to the amusement

or indifference of those before

me who succeeded

Someone has taken

to chalking the word ACTIVIST on the castle

walls and erasing it   from which blur

emerges the face of Gudrun Ensslin

as Gerhard Richter renders her   beaming

geckolike into an ecstatic

future   In some countries

instead of *police lineup*

they say *identity parade*

In others instead of *not guilty*

they say *not proven*

In general instead of *victim*

we say *survivor* unless

the survivor did not

Form becomes content

and together they step forward

to accept the prize   The prize

is light   but has what I've ever done

been enough to earn it

The other day I saw some ants

carrying a dragonfly's head

away from its body

with the astonishing air

of consensus it seems only ants possess

We tell ourselves

that what a dragonfly sees

looks like what we see

when at the concert everyone holds up

their phones to prove to each other

that they are together

       When I checked

a few minutes later the dragonfly's body

was gone and the head

was still there

Ant consensus apparently was

you know what guys

forget the head

a body's what we need

///

It's halfway through October 2017
and today New York woke up finally
to what feels
like it could be fall and the news
that a school district in Mississippi
is banning *To Kill a Mockingbird* again
        and nobody
                because white people
                are quadrupling down
                so spectacularly on their bullshit this year
        is surprised

Last week I quoted someone
out of context about irony
and in doing so probably
made myself some extra enemies
Later my friend mentioned
tenor and vehicle
the two components of metaphor
but it's no use I can never remember
which is which   I'm afraid
I don't respond
to stimuli in the way
I'm supposed to

I tried looking up
the size of a blue whale's heart

and it turns out no it's not

as big as a small car after all

but the National Geographic website

reassures everyone that it's *still pretty big*

and that *the blue whale's heart*

needs a better metaphor

The website asks

How big is your own heart

When we find out

that the president has made a joke

about the vice president wanting

to hang all the gays

our hearts are not surprised

nor is it exactly surprise I read

on the apostle Thomas's face

where Caravaggio has painted

him slipping   with Jesus's help

one finger into the hole

in Jesus's side   a hole that resembles

other things that also are holes

We're told it's doubt that drives

Thomas and perhaps that's close enough

It looks like he's about

to stroke

the human heart

of Jesus   but for the fact

that the hole is on the wrong side

///

What is missing from the trees
What is missing from a life
    color sucked from the spines
    of books by the sun

When I look into my life I cannot name
the trees but when I touch the books
on my shelf it's as if I might
feel the trees in them

Where are the people who would have heard me
call you by any of the nicknames
I had for you and what
would I by any of them be called

Would I be called *witness*
a word that in Greek is the same
as the word for martyr
one for me and one for you

From here I can picture almost
dispassionately a book whose cover
shows the shadows of both of us
exchanging places in this word

///

One night John Ashbery came over

for dinner and I had on

The Disintegration Loops which he guessed

was Brian Eno which is an excellent guess

   Later he praised

the potatoes dauphinoise

that I had made without realizing

that's what they were called

John and I were both from upstate New York

so one of the first times we met we gossiped

about which weathermen on the local news

we thought were handsomest up there

The day John died I was stuck

in a motel technically in Provincetown

but less than a hundred feet

from the Truro sign

In my suitcase was a copy

of *Self-Portrait in a Convex Mirror*

so I took it to the beach in the rain

and read from random

pages to the mist and the gulls

   "Father I thought we'd lost you
   In the blue and buff planes of the Aegean:
   Now it seems you're really back."
   "Only for a while, son, only for a while."
   We can go inside now.

It was the smallest my voice
had sounded to me in years
though maybe that's what let the wind
carry it farther

Walking back across the beach
to the hotel I saw
a dead horseshoe crab
that from even a short distance
seemed like it could have been
alive but who can tell with
such an ancient thing
The corpse looked like it was made
of hammered gold
covered in sand and wax

I walked away from it
I went inside

///

In case what Yoko Ono said is true

       that to name one's enemy in one's art

       injures the art more than the enemy

I won't tell you who

is president now

       I forget the name of the woman

who gave you acupuncture but not

of your ex-lover who   mornings

toward the end   washed you

when you could no longer walk

to the bathroom

We argued over which of us

would give you your sponge bath

each morning   I ended up

able to bear it once

I forget who brought

to your hospital room

a single gardenia blossom

because you loved Billie Holiday

but I haven't forgotten the name

of the man who at the party after

the reception after your memorial

flung himself into a fit of wailing

next to the margarita machine

       He wailed out of grief over you

and because as we would learn

but did not yet know

       he had it too

For years I would say magnolia

when I meant gardenia

and would flinch whenever I smelled one

           all sweetness and rot

How many thousands

of stories like yours

have been told

and forgotten   how many

stories of lovingly durable nurses

      of hospital sheets   of IV tubes

      dripping saline and morphine

How many stories of drugs

that would haul you

along in their wake for a while

but finally

let you sink   How many versions

of your scrotum

becoming so swollen

that the only thing I could think of

as I dabbed it one morning

with a washcloth

was a grapefruit

then couldn't eat grapefruit for years

///

After a thunderstorm
a writer told a chapel full of people
about the time he showed his brother
the story he was about to read to us
What it was about I can't
recall   something terrible
and meaningful to both of them
and probably to those of us who had
assembled in the chapel
to soak up terror and meaning
              or at least to extract
some of the latter from the former

After reading it   his brother
              had gone out to walk his dog
with the story still in his pocket
Lacking anything suitable he used
some of the pages to scoop up
the dog's shit from the sidewalk

I've never felt I've known
a story well enough to make
such practical use of it

In August of 2001 I was walking
with poets in Copenhagen
and we encountered on the sidewalk
a smallish pile of dog shit

into the center of which

a handwritten note had been stuck

Maybe one of us decided

it was a poem

Whatever it said we couldn't read it

written   as it was   in Danish

and though at least one of us

considered it   no way

were we going to pluck it out

and bring it back

for our new Danish friends

to translate

Out of the body come

the usual questions

      How are we supposed to tell

the difference between stories and poems

between author   and speaker

between terror and meaning

between owners   and dogs

      between all of us living

      and all of us dead

///

Twenty years after you died
I am still seeing sometimes
around Manhattan one of your exes
      also named Mark
         because that's how our story
            has always told itself

Mark and his dogs lived
in the same building downtown
as my friends and their dogs   I assume
he didn't recognize me
and what would I even have said
as we passed in the lobby
        Hi you might not remember me but

Recently Mark and I ended
up seated at adjacent tables
at a restaurant in the Village
where I lacked the nerve to bring myself
to lean over to my friend
and say   *Don't look*
         but that guy over there

My friend had been talking about
colony collapse and poetries
of witness but I was too distracted
to listen   I felt like a bee
who'd been heading

for honey and gotten trapped instead

in tar

Recently I read that saving the honeybees

would no more save all the bees

than saving the chickens would

save all the birds

     I often confuse

     a sense of futility

     with a call to action

An artist places broken

figurines in beehives

and the bees build their honeycombs

on them mending and mutating

the shards

Grief operates like that

its collaborators unwitting unaware

of the work being done

Grief arrives as shadows

   of bees

darkening hives of loss

///

A poet had just taken

his own life and a group of us

met to see how everything

was going to feel   a humid night

a glass of wine   another's hair against

our skin when we hugged

on the sidewalk outside the bar

where we had assembled to compare

the size and shape

as we experienced it

of this poet-shaped hole

newly gouged into our lives

I was older than most of those

who were there that night

One woman told me that

at twenty-three she had

never before lost anyone

not a parent

not a grandparent

I flashed to myself at her age

my stupid hair and baggy jeans

and of the friends around me dying

and all the strange species

of luck that in any of us evolve

///

Let the balloons go outside.

Let the balloons go outside.

—Trish Keenan

Not long ago the pope decreed

that unbaptized babies would

no longer be banished to Limbo

and that their little souls languishing

there would be released

Imagine them getting the papal memo

and rising in unison   unsure

of where to go

except up   twirling like colossal flocks

of river martins

in dark enormous coils   their outlines

becoming eventually lighter

then translucent   then clear

We might guess incorrectly

that the accompanying sound

would be the usual celestial

harps and choirs

instead of the intolerable shriek

that trapped breath makes

when it escapes from a balloon

whose opening is being pulled taut

           or tens of thousands of these

Sebastião Salgado talks about traveling

through parts of Brazil

where babies died so frequently

that churches rented out coffins for their funerals

and reused them dozens of times

A local vendor might sell bananas

and ice cream alongside shoes in which

babies could be buried

       Salgado also says that when

babies end up in Limbo

it has something to do with whether

or not their eyes are open or closed

when they are buried

                or is it when they die   I'm not sure

     The transcription

of the interview is unclear

When someone in a movie dies

with their eyes open

the lids are made to look

so easy to close

A priest for instance or a doctor

passes a reverent hand

over the corpse's face

perhaps not even touching it

and the task is complete

The morning you died
our friend and your brother and I were
in your bed with your body
that overnight had decided
it was no longer you
but some awful machine
designed to lurch and wheeze
until it sucked in one
more breath and did not let it out

Your eyes were open and when
after a few minutes
no one came to close them
I tried to do it myself
but the lids kept popping back open
like busted window shades

The word limbo derives from the Latin
word *limbus*   a border   an edge
It also is a dance   that also is a contest
in which the winning dancer
is the one who doesn't fall

///

This year I should turn fifty

twice as old as you were when you died

One night the year before you were born

the Arno flooded the city of Florence

and now when people walk

down certain Florentine streets

or into certain churches or museums

they can still see a smudge several feet

above their heads

often with a small plaque

next to it to indicate

that this was the level the water reached

There are days when everything

feels like a metaphor

for your having died

There are days

when nothing does

///

In one of the *Star Trek* movies the crew goes back

in time to our time to save the whales

Along the way they have to retrieve

one of their injured number

from a hospital and the *Enterprise*'s

crotchety doctor is disgusted

by the crude equipment

and barbaric treatments

to which the patients

are being subjected

He asks one of them what her illness is

                    kidney disease

and with an eyeroll

he pulls from his pocket a pill

that cures the afflicted woman

How many of us

in the theater wanted

to reach through the darkness

for that pill on the screen

How many of us just wanted

to touch the doctor's hand

///

After you died we took what was left
out of your apartment   To me
came a few stray objects
a book   a pair of dumbbells
photo album   shoes
Maybe some clothes
went to charity   everything else
you'd already given away

Once when I came back to town
after you died I slept at the home
of the man you had left me for
and who years later you'd leave for me
give or take some others in between

I saw what you might have seen
in him   a steady job
in catering I think
        or maybe family money
hair that behaved
and a big apartment with a piano
he could play
Even if we felt desire we didn't
let it roll us into each other
as we slept or pretended to sleep
together in his king-size bed
Why had we done that

Was there no couch

I could have slept on instead

In his bathroom closet

he had numerous tubes

of toothpaste   rows of boxes of kleenex

antiperspirants bought in bulk   It struck

me as at once decadent and frugal

but why not

when someone has room

for such things and foresees

living long enough to use them

///

I wish I still had some
of your ashes
so I could throw them on
the White House lawn   We had plotted
with you about dropping them
from a hot-air balloon but we ended
up instead in a tiny airplane that felt
more cramped than a Volkswagen Bug
as we flew low over the rippling mountains
the greens of the pines
below us sturdy and real

We were the same three
who had been in the bed with you
when you died   plus the pilot
who in piloting
our mission was probably
risking a significant fine

I don't know which of us was holding
the bag that contained what remained
of you but when we tried to shake you out
a bunch of you blew back in
making the inside of the plane
look briefly like a snow globe

How strange the bits that landed

on my tongue didn't taste

of anything that could ever have burned

///

When David Markson died
all of his books with his
annotations in the margins
were boxed up and sent
            to his favorite bookstore
where the staff released them
into the wilds of the shelves
Don Quixote   Don DeLillo
Heidegger and wretched old Pound

Word went out   in the ways
in which it does now
and a kind of scavenger hunt began
            Markson's books drifting off like leaves
on a hundred breezes
to land in a hundred strangers' libraries
                  his marginalia becoming
an untethered archive
            an elegy both fracturing
            and perpetuating itself

Borges could have written
the story of this story
            in which a writer dies and his books
are bought by strangers
and taken away   then decades later

after the last stranger dies

word again goes out

in the ways in which it will

and all the books come back together

      all the books come back

///

I was looking for a song for you
and in looking found two others
but neither was the one
                                 I had in mind
We were in a room of gorgeous noise
together then we weren't
It was not sad though I wanted you
to come back
                       Should I have
said searching instead of looking
for instance in grade school
if a friend reaching
for what I was holding
said let me see that   I'd say you see
with your eyes not with your hands
and pull whatever it was away
          I was clever
in a severely limited sense
                      synesthesia and synecdoche
could have been distant
afflictions for all I knew and still I find
too many ways to grab
a world or what was lost
from it with no way finally
capable of doing so
completely enough for me

The song I still am looking for

is a song without words my favorite

kind lately not because words

are precious and not because I live

already in them even though

they are and I do

Someone said writing about music

is like dancing about architecture

and I have no real gift for description you

already know how charmed every time

I was by your charming hat

which I won't describe

here except to say that touching it

felt like touching you

What if I could tell you I was striking

with someone else's hands

a drum made of pure light

and that I could find the sounds

my striking made

only at the unraveling edge

of sleep where they dissolved

into the competing noise

made every morning

by terrible jaws of sunlight opening

to swallow a song I could never

hold for long but wanted you nevertheless

and always to see

///

The book's epigraph is from the "Rooms" section of Gertrude Stein's *Tender Buttons*.

15 [When I was a teenager I smugly told] Paul Celan and Virginia Woolf committed suicide by drowning in the rivers Seine and Ouse, respectively.

25 [From here I can see a fountain] The epigraph is from Mary Jo Bang's "The Role of Elegy" in *Elegy*.

30 [When finally everyone was granted their childhood] "Two Feet off the Ground" is the title of a song by Thom Yorke.

36 [I have been terrified] The quote is from C.D. Wright's "By Jude Jean McCramack / Goddamnit to Hell Dog's Foot" in *Cooling Time: An American Poetry Vigil*.

40 [Here in the spectral academy] The quote is from *Candy Darling: Memoirs of an Andy Warhol Superstar*.

42 [Inverted wooden tables] Doris Salcedo retrospective, Guggenheim Museum, New York City, 2015.

43 [Not often but sometimes I look] The song "God Bless the Child" was written by Billie Holiday and Arthur Herzog Jr. in 1939.

48 [The night David Wojnarowicz died] American artist and activist David Wojnarowicz died of AIDS in 1992 at the age of 37. The phrase "little ounce" is from Lucie Brock-Broido's "For a Snow Leopard in October" in *Stay, Illusion*.

58 [There are many ways to get] The Gerhard Richter painting is *Gegenüberstellung 2 (Confrontation 2)*, 1988.

60 [It's halfway through October 2017] The Caravaggio painting is *The Incredulity of Saint Thomas*, c. 1601–1602.

64 [One night John Ashbery came over] The quote is from John Ashbery's "The Tomb of Stuart Merrill" in *Self-Portrait in a Convex Mirror*.

70 [Twenty years after you died] The artist referenced is Aganetha Dyck (after an article by Sarah Zhang, "An Artist and Her Bees Create Beautiful Honeycomb-Draped Sculptures," on the *Gizmodo* website).

73 [Not long ago the pope decreed] The epigraph quotes the song "Lunch Hour Pops," from the 2003 album *Haha Sound*, by Broadcast. Lyrics by Trish Keenan (1968–2011). *The Salt of the Earth* is a 2014 documentary about photographer Sebastião Salgado, directed by Juliano Ribeiro Salgado and Wim Wenders.

76 [This year I should turn fifty] The epigraph is from a plaque near the entrance to the Spanish Chapel in Museo Santa Maria di Novella, Florence, and translates roughly as "on November 4, 1966, water from the Arno reached this height."

82 [When David Markson died] David Markson (1927–2010) was the author of *Wittgenstein's Mistress, Reader's Block,* and other novels.

ACKNOWLEDGMENTS

My sincere thanks to everyone who has been supportive of this book, including the editors of the following: the Academy of American Poets' Poem-a-Day, *DIAGRAM*, *Guernica*, *Lemon Hound*, *Narrative*, *The Ocean State Review*, *Poetry*, *A Public Space*, *VOLT*.

An earlier version of [Here in the spectral academy] appeared in *T Magazine* (the *New York Times*) accompanied by a collage entitled "Candy Ruins" by Rachel Feinstein.

An earlier version of [There are many ways to get] appeared in *Dear Another*, which accompanied an exhibition of paintings and collages by Jessica Rankin.

Extra love and gratitude to Mary Jo Bang, who read the manuscript and suggested several helpful edits, and to the marvelous crew at Copper Canyon.

ABOUT THE AUTHOR

Mark Bibbins is the author of three previous books: *They Don't Kill You Because They're Hungry, They Kill You Because They're Full*; *The Dance of No Hard Feelings*; and *Sky Lounge,* which received a Lambda Literary Award. Bibbins teaches in the graduate writing programs of The New School and Columbia University and in NYU's Writers in Florence program. He lives in New York City.

Lannan Literary Selections

For two decades Lannan Foundation has supported the publication and distribution of exceptional literary works. Copper Canyon Press gratefully acknowledges their support.

LANNAN LITERARY SELECTIONS 2020

Mark Bibbins, *13th Balloon*

Victoria Chang, *Obit*

Leila Chatti, *Deluge*

Philip Metres, *Shrapnel Maps*

Natalie Shapero, *Popular Longing*

RECENT LANNAN LITERARY SELECTIONS FROM COPPER CANYON PRESS

Sherwin Bitsui, *Dissolve*

Jericho Brown, *The Tradition*

John Freeman, *Maps*

Jenny George, *The Dream of Reason*

Ha Jin, *A Distant Center*

Deborah Landau, *Soft Targets*

Maurice Manning, *One Man's Dark*

Rachel McKibbens, *blud*

Aimee Nezhukumatathil, *Oceanic*

Camille Rankine, *Incorrect Merciful Impulses*

Paisley Rekdal, *Nightingale*

Natalie Scenters-Zapico, *Lima :: Limón*

Frank Stanford, *What About This: Collected Poems of Frank Stanford*

Ocean Vuong, *Night Sky with Exit Wounds*

C.D. Wright, *Casting Deep Shade*

Javier Zamora, *Unaccompanied*

Matthew Zapruder, *Father's Day*

Ghassan Zaqtan (translated by Fady Joudah), *The Silence That Remains*

Poetry is vital to language and living. Since 1972, Copper Canyon Press has published extraordinary poetry from around the world to engage the imaginations and intellects of readers, writers, booksellers, librarians, teachers, students, and donors.

WE ARE GRATEFUL FOR THE MAJOR SUPPORT PROVIDED BY:

THE PAUL G. ALLEN
FAMILY FOUNDATION

Lannan

A&

OFFICE OF ARTS & CULTURE

SEATTLE

WASHINGTON STATE
ARTS COMMISSION

TO LEARN MORE ABOUT UNDERWRITING
COPPER CANYON PRESS TITLES,
PLEASE CALL 360-385-4925 EXT. 103

WE ARE GRATEFUL FOR THE MAJOR SUPPORT PROVIDED BY:

Anonymous

Jill Baker and Jeffrey Bishop

Anne and Geoffrey Barker

Donna and Matt Bellew

Diana Broze

John R. Cahill

The Beatrice R. and Joseph A.
Coleman Foundation Inc.

The Currie Family Fund

Laurie and Oskar Eustis

Saramel and Austin Evans

Mimi Gardner Gates

Gull Industries Inc. on behalf of
William True

The Trust of Warren A. Gummow

Carolyn and Robert Hedin

Bruce Kahn

Phil Kovacevich and Eric Wechsler

Lakeside Industries Inc. on behalf
of Jeanne Marie Lee

Maureen Lee and Mark Busto

Peter Lewis

Ellie Mathews and Carl Youngmann
as The North Press

Larry Mawby

Hank Meijer

Jack Nicholson

Petunia Charitable Fund and
adviser Elizabeth Hebert

Gay Phinny

Suzie Rapp and Mark Hamilton

Emily and Dan Raymond

Jill and Bill Ruckelshaus

Cynthia Sears

Kim and Jeff Seely

Dan Waggoner

Randy and Joanie Woods

Barbara and Charles Wright

Caleb Young as C. Young Creative

The dedicated interns and
faithful volunteers of
Copper Canyon Press

The Chinese character for poetry is made up of two parts:
"word" and "temple." It also serves as pressmark for
Copper Canyon Press.

The poems are set in Verdigris Pro.
Book design and composition by Phil Kovacevich.